The Tower Clock

and

How to Make It

———

A Practical and Theoretical Treatise on the Construction
of a Chiming Tower Clock, with Full Working
Drawings Photographed to Scale.

———

By E. B. Ferson, A. M., Mass.

Instructor In drawing and machine design in The Chicago Manual
Training School of The University of Chicago.

British Library Cataloguing-in-Publication Data
A catalogue record for this book is available from the
British Library

A History of Clocks and Watches

Horology (from the Latin, Horologium) is the science of measuring time. Clocks, watches, clockwork, sundials, clepsydras, timers, time recorders, marine chronometers and atomic clocks are all examples of instruments used to measure time. In current usage, horology refers mainly to the study of mechanical time-keeping devices, whilst chronometry more broadly included electronic devices that have largely supplanted mechanical clocks for accuracy and precision in time-keeping. Horology itself has an incredibly long history and there are many museums and several specialised libraries devoted to the subject. Perhaps the most famous is the *Royal Greenwich Observatory*, also the source of the Prime Meridian (longitude 0° 0' 0"), and the home of the first marine timekeepers accurate enough to determine longitude.

The word 'clock' is derived from the Celtic words *clagan* and *clocca* meaning 'bell'. A silent instrument missing such a mechanism has traditionally been known as a timepiece, although today the words have become interchangeable. The clock is one of the oldest human interventions, meeting the need to consistently measure intervals of time shorter than the natural units: the day, the lunar month and the year. The current sexagesimal system of time measurement dates to approximately 2000 BC in Sumer. The Ancient Egyptians divided the day into two twelve-hour periods and used large obelisks to track the movement of the sun. They also developed water clocks, which had also been employed frequently by the Ancient Greeks, who called them 'clepsydrae'. The Shang Dynasty is also believed to have used the outflow water clock around the same time.

The first mechanical clocks, employing the verge escapement mechanism (the mechanism that controls the rate of a clock by advancing the gear train at regular intervals or 'ticks') with a foliot or balance wheel timekeeper (a weighted wheel that rotates back and forth, being returned toward its centre position by a spiral), were invented in Europe at around the start of the fourteenth century. They became the standard timekeeping device until the pendulum clock was invented in 1656. This remained the most accurate timekeeper until the 1930s, when quartz oscillators (where the mechanical **resonance** of a vibrating crystal is used to create an electrical signal with a very precise **frequency**) were invented, followed by atomic clocks after World War Two. Although initially limited to laboratories, the development of microelectronics in the 1960s made **quartz clocks** both compact and cheap to produce, and by the 1980s they became the world's dominant timekeeping technology in both clocks and **wristwatches**.

The concept of the wristwatch goes back to the production of the very earliest watches in the sixteenth century. Elizabeth I of England received a wristwatch from Robert Dudley in 1571, described as an arm watch. From the beginning, they were almost exclusively worn by women, while men used pocket-watches up until the early twentieth century. This was not just a matter of fashion or prejudice; watches of the time were notoriously prone to fouling from exposure to the elements, and could only reliably be kept safe from harm if carried securely in the pocket. Wristwatches were first worn by military men towards the end of the nineteenth century, when the importance of synchronizing manoeuvres during war without potentially revealing the plan to the enemy through signalling was increasingly recognized. It was clear that using pocket watches while in the heat of battle or while mounted on a horse was impractical, so officers began to strap the watches to their wrist.

The company H. Williamson Ltd., based in Coventry, England, was one of the first to capitalize on this opportunity. During the company's 1916 AGM it was noted that '...the public is buying the practical things of life. Nobody can truthfully contend that the watch is a luxury. It is said that one soldier in every four wears a wristlet watch, and the other three mean to get one as soon as they can.' By the end of the War, almost all enlisted men wore a wristwatch, and after they were demobilized, the fashion soon caught on - the British *Horological Journal* wrote in 1917 that '...the wristlet watch was little used by the sterner sex before the war, but now is seen on the wrist of nearly every man in uniform and of many men in civilian attire.' Within a decade, sales of wristwatches had outstripped those of pocket watches.

Now that clocks and watches had become 'common objects' there was a massively increased demand on clockmakers for maintenance and repair. Julien Le Roy, a clockmaker of Versailles, invented a face that could be opened to view the inside clockwork – a development which many subsequent artisans copied. He also invented special repeating mechanisms to improve the precision of clocks and supervised over 3,500 watches. The more complicated the device however, the more often it needed repairing. Today, since almost all clocks are now factory-made, most modern clockmakers *only* repair clocks. They are frequently employed by jewellers, antique shops or places devoted strictly to repairing clocks and watches.

The clockmakers of the present must be able to read blueprints and instructions for numerous types of clocks and time pieces that vary from antique clocks to modern time pieces in order to fix and make clocks or watches. The trade requires fine motor coordination as clockmakers must frequently work on devices with small gears and fine machinery, as well as an appreciation for the original art form. As is evident from this very short history of clocks and watches, over the centuries the items themselves have changed – almost out of recognition, but the importance of time-keeping has not. It is an area which provides a constant source of fascination and scientific discovery, still very much evolving today. We hope the reader enjoys this book.

PREFACE.

A number of volumes might be written on the subject of clocks and bells, and their history. The subject matter is very interesting reading; but this is not a history of clock making. It is only a description of a clock which has been built for the University of Chicago by pupils of the Chicago Manual Training School, boys ranging from 14 to 18 years of age. The theoretical and time calculations were made by the instructor; but the drawings, patterns and machine work are the work of the boys. The assembled drawings of the clock shown in Figs. 1 and 2, are the personal work of the whole Senior class of about 45 pupils, each one of whom had a particular part assigned to him; and after that part had been drawn in detail, it was put in its proper place in these drawings by the pupil who had made it, so that the assembled drawings are the composite work of the class.

A part of our course in drawing and machine design is the designing and building of some machine, and this clock is one in a list of machines which includes steam engines from six to ten horse power, a heavy drill press, a steam hammer, a cutter grinder and numerous other machine tools for the shops.

E. B. Ferson

SPECIFICATIONS OF THE CLOCK.

The clock was designed from a purely mechanical standpoint and without any preconceived or sentimental ideas, but simply as a machine to keep time, the object being to do the work accurately with the least possible number of parts and those parts of the simplest form. For the reasons above stated it was decided to build the clock as three separate machines to be mounted on a common bed-plate.

First, a time part, which should furnish power to drive the visible time-keepers; i. e., the hands on the dials.

Second, a striking part, to give the time on the hour bell, and third, a chime part to give the musical quarters on four smaller bells. This arrangement of parts is a decided advantage, for in case anything should happen to any one of the parts, that part may be disconnected, and the necessary repairs made without any interference with the other parts.

Perhaps the quickest way to get to our subject would be to follow the preacher's method and give you a text, which in this case would be the specifications for the clock. They are as follows:

1. To make and set a clock with four dials of 12 feet diameter, striking the hours and Westminster quarters on bells which would be the second, third, fourth, seventh and tenor of a peal of eight, the tenor to weigh 7,000 pounds.

2. The dials to be illuminated, with the figures and minutes of cast-iron in rings; the body of the dial to be of opal glass of 22 ounces per square foot. There must be no straight radial bars from the center. There must be a clear

opening in the wall the full diameter of the dial, and no ledge upon which snow or ice can collect.

3. The minute hands to have a short external counter-poise, painted the same color as the dial; the hands, figures and minutes to be black, and the framework of the dial gilt.

4. The escapement to be a Sir Edmund Beckett's double three-legged gravity.

5. The pendulum to have a cast-iron jar with steel tube; mercury compensation; to beat seconds and swing two and one-half degrees from 0 or a total arc of five degrees.

6. The clock to rest on steel I-beams entirely independent of the floor of the clock room. The pendulum cock to rise from the clock frame.

7. There must be a minute dial, and a dial for seconds.

8. The time part to have an independent maintaining power to keep it in motion while being wound, and to be so designed that it will run eight days.

9. The striking parts to be wound up every day. The fourth quarter bell to have two hammers.

10. The striking of the hours to let off independently of the quarters, and the first blow of the hour struck exactly on the hour; the other quarters to begin exactly at 15, 30 and 45 minutes.

11. The hour hammer to be not less than one-sixtieth of the weight of the bell, and be raised not less than nine inches; the quarters' hammers to increase in weight from a sixtieth to a fortieth of the weight of their bells. The small hammers to be raised not less than six inches.

12.. The large going wheels and the larger pinions to be cast-iron, the small pinions of steel, and all bushings of brass.

13. The winding barrels to be of cast-iron of sufficient thickness to withstand the compression caused by the rope in winding; the rope used to be a one-fourth inch steel rope, which *must not* be wound more than one layer on the wheel.

14. The flies to be at the back of the clock, and long enough to make the intervals between strokes uniform and sufficiently great.

15. All the metal except working surfaces to be painted University maroon.

16. There must be something to warn or stop the winding; and also a box about three feet deep filled with small stone to catch the weights if they fall.

17. All shafts to be made to take out separately by unscrewing the bushings.

18. The clock to be enclosed in a room as near air-tight as possible, to keep out dust and avoid sudden changes of temperature.

THE TIME TRAIN.

For the time train a quarter inch wire rope on the barrel, four turns in each 24 hours, for eight days, gives a barrel, No. 1, eight inches long; and with two extra turns for careless winding makes it eight and one-half inches long, which is a convenient length. On the shaft with this goes the great wheel, No. 2, of 120 teeth, which will turn once in six hours; this must not be keyed to the going shaft, but is to be driven by ratchet teeth on one end of the barrel and a pawl attached to one of the arms of the great wheel. The winding wheel, No. 4, and the drum, are keyed to the going shaft.

The winding pinion, No. 3, is on a shaft, the end of which is squared to fit the key; this pinion is made to slide on a feather key in the shaft, so that it can be thrown out of gear when not winding.

The maintaining power, Fig. 3, consists of a shaft, A, a straight lever, B, a segment of a pinion, C, a curved, double lever, D, a weight E. The shaft, A, slides endwise to engage the teeth of the pinion segment with the teeth of the great wheel, No. 2, the straight lever has a handle at both ends to assist in throwing the pinion out or in and a shield at the outer end to cover the end of the winding shaft, No. 3, when the key is not on it.

The curved lever is double, and the pinion segment turns loosely between the halves, and on the shaft, A; it is held up in its place by a light spring, F; the weight, E, is also held between the two halves of the double lever.

(8)

The action is as follows: The end of the lever, B, covers the end of the winding shaft so that it is necessary to raise it before putting the key on the winding shaft; it is raised

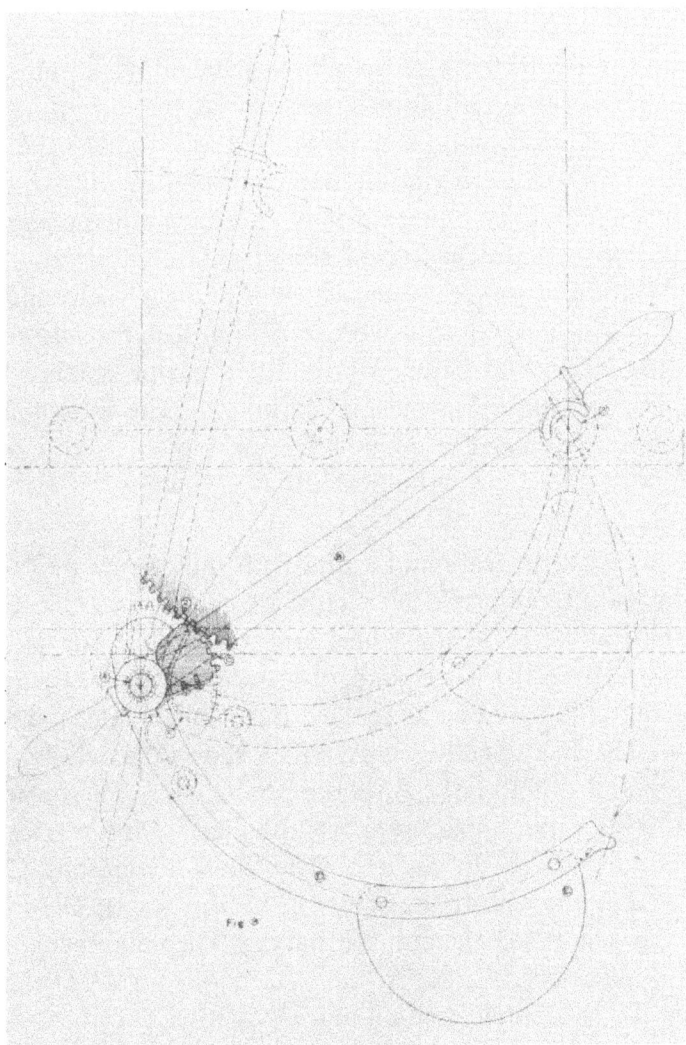

Fig 3.

till it strikes a stop, and then pushed in till the pinion seg-ment engages with the going wheel of the train, when the weight, E, acting through the levers, furnishes power to drive the clock-train while the going weight is being wound up. Of course the weight on the maintaining power must be so proportioned to the leverage that it will be equal to the power of the going barrel and its weight, a simple proposition in mechanics.

The number of teeth on the pinion segment, C, is sufficient to maintain power for fifteen minutes, at the end of which time the lever, B, will come down and again cover the end of the winding shaft; or, it may be pumped out of gear and dropped down. In case it is forgotten, the spring, F, will allow the segment to pass out of gear of itself and will simply allow it to give a click as it slips over each tooth in the going wheel; if this were not provided for, it would stop the clock. As before stated, the great or going wheel has 120 teeth and turns once in six hours. The second shaft in the train, being the hour shaft, the pinion, No. 6 must have 20 teeth. On the hour shaft, No. 5 are:

First, the dial gears and a dial with the minute and hour hands, to set the clock by. This, of course, has the usual gears of 45 teeth in the wheel and 15 teeth in the pinion, and 48 teeth in the wheel, and 12 teeth in the pinion in order to change the speed so as to give the minutes and hours on the setting dial. See Fig. 1-A, which shows the detail of the setting-dial. The shaft, A, is the hour shaft. The bushing, B, with its studs, a, b, c, supports the dial, C, and carries the change gears, E, F, G, H. The shaft extension, D, is screwed to the end of the shaft, A, by the screw, D[1], forming the arbor for the minute hand. The minute hand is held in place on its arbor by the head of the screw, D[1]. The arbor, D, also carries the pinion, E, of fifteen teeth, driving the wheel, F, of forty-five teeth, which is carried on the stud, c, being mounted on the hub of the pinion, G, of twelve teeth, which, in turn, drives the wheel of forty-eight teeth whose hub forms the arbor for the hour hand, revolving once in twelve hours.

Second, a pair of bevel gears, No. 7 (for leading off bevels to the large dials), of 44 and 48 teeth respectively, of which we shall say more later on.

Third, the second wheel in the train, of 105 teeth, No. 8. The hub of this wheel revolves on a steel bushing, E, shown

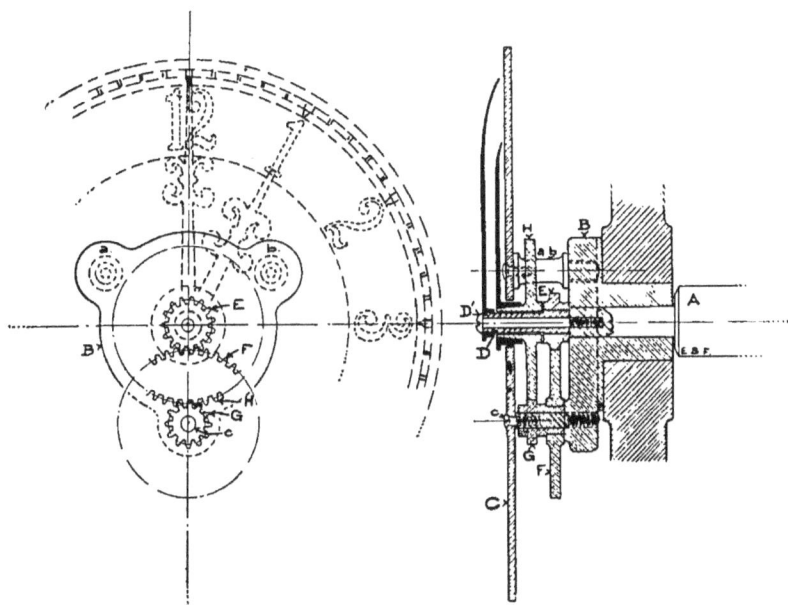

Fig. 1a. Details of Dial and Motion Work on Clock.

in Fig. 4, which is keyed to the shaft. On one side of the rim of the wheel, A, are cut 60 grooves or teeth, one for each minute, to use in setting the hands on the large dials to one minute; the space, B, is 6 degrees, and the set screws, C and C¹, make the lever, D, adjustable to seconds for the finer setting of the minute hands, so that they will correspond exactly to the striking parts. The set screws which control the lever, D, have 20 threads per inch; the angular movement for one minute at the center of the screws, C and C¹, is equal to .1875 inches; one second angular movement therefore equals .003125 inches. One revolution of the

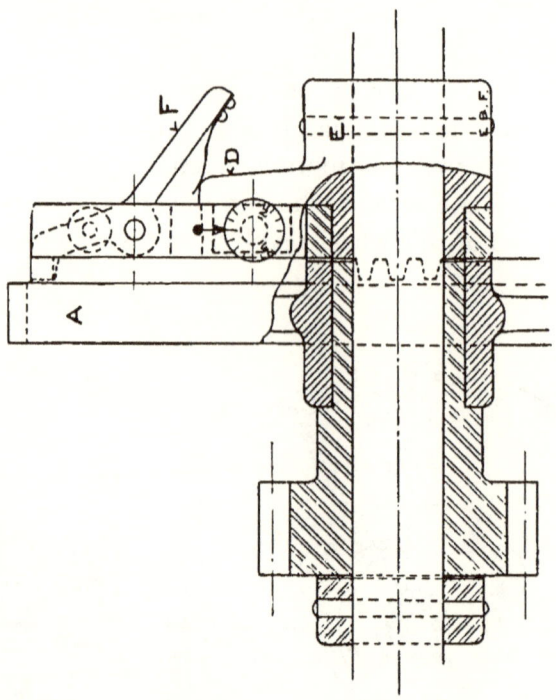

Fig. 4.

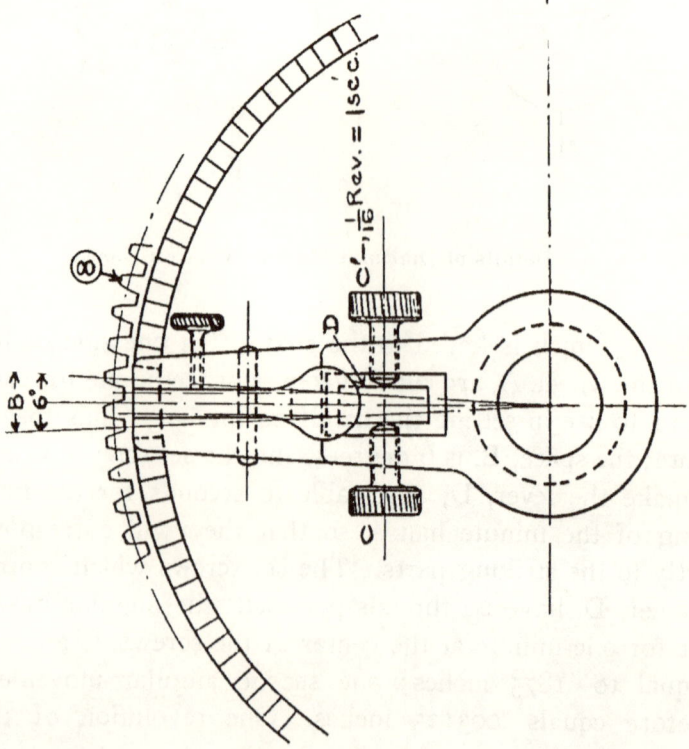

screw equals .05 inches; therefore, one second angular movement calls for one-sixteenth revolution of a screw of 20 threads, and the heads of the screws, C and C¹, are for that reason divided on their edges into 16 parts.

In Fig. 4, the wheel, A, which is shown as being mounted upon the sleeve of the hub, E, should be carried on the sleeve of the pinion, No. 6, Figs. 1 and 2, so that when setting the hands on the dials, the time train will not be interfered with in its movement. The arrangement above described takes the place of the friction-tight center arbor in a watch or smaller clock, as by pressing down on the lever, F, until the teeth on the side of wheel, A, Fig. 4, (or wheel 8 of the time train), are disengaged the hour shaft may then be rotated independently of the time train. This is done when setting the clock roughly while the finer adjustments are made by the adjusting screws C and C'.

To put this in plain figures: .1875 divided by .05 equals 3.75 revolutions. Sixty divided by 3.75 equals 16, or one-sixteenth revolution.

Fourth, the dropping wheel, No. 9, or cam, with a pin, No. 11, on one side of it, for the usual warning before the strike. The final drop is done upon the proper second by the cam, or snail, j, on the wheel, No. 10, which revolves once in 15 minutes. On the other side of the wheel, No. 9, are four pins, a¹, a², a³, a⁴, which give the warning of the quarters, and on the face of the wheel, No. 9, are four cams, f¹, f², f³, f⁴, which drop at their proper intervals. See Fig. 14. On the third shaft are:

First, the driving pinion, No. 11, of 14 teeth, giving seven and one-half revolutions of this shaft per hour, or eight minutes for one revolution.

Second, the third wheel, No. 13, of 120 teeth.

Third, a wheel, No. 12, of 48 teeth, driving one of 90 teeth, No. 10, on a shaft above, giving one revolution in 15 minutes. A cam, J, Fig. 11, on the side of this wheel gives the final drop of the hour striking lever.

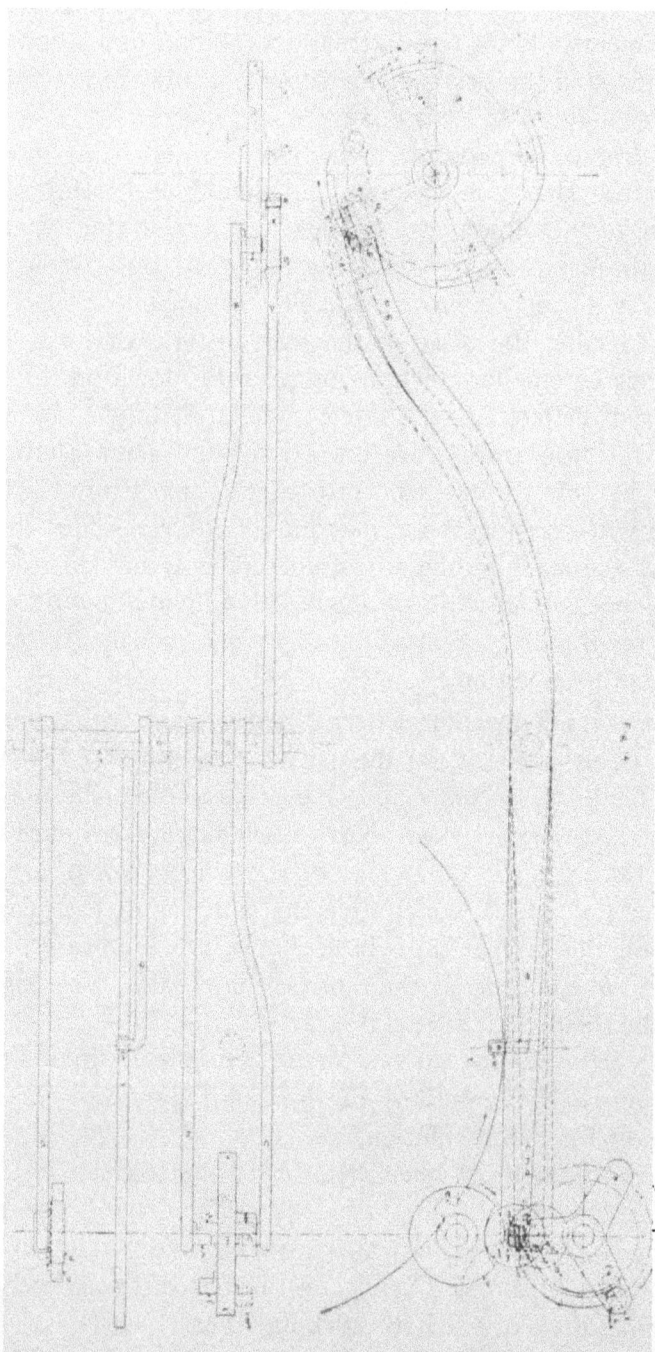

On the fourth shaft are:

First, The driven pinion, No. 14, of 15 teeth, giving one revolution per minute, and to the end of this shaft is affixed a hand to mark seconds on a dial which is made upon the bushing of the shaft; this dial is divided to read seconds.

Second, The fourth wheel, No. 15, of 120 teeth.

The fifth shaft is the escapement shaft with its pinion, No. 16, of 12 teeth, giving one revolution in six seconds.

There is upon this shaft the escapement fly, Fig. 6, with vanes or fans as long as it is possible to make them; length is more important than width in any mechanism of this kind, as it is the *length* of the *leverage,* rather than the *surface* exposed to the pressure of the air, which equalizes the motion and softens the blow of the legs of the escapement on the pallets. This shaft is short, as all the parts must be small, and the shaft would not be stiff enough to stand all the strains put upon it, if it was made of the same length as the others.

The escapement is the double three-legged, gravity escapement, invented by Sir Edmund Beckett, the eminent English authority on clock design, and designer of the great Westminster clock in London, whose general specifications I have followed in the design of this clock.

Referring to Fig. 5, this escapement is so called because it has two three-legged wheels, A, B, C, and a, b, c, which are placed in different planes, with a set of three lifting pins, D, between them.

The two wheels must be squared upon the arbor, so that there will be no possibility of slipping. They are made from heavy sheet steel, with the ends of the arms hardened. The lifting pins, D, are shouldered between them, like a three-toothed lantern pinion.

Referring to the enlarged detail in the lower right-hand corner of Fig. 5, the shaded portion shows the form which has been decided upon for the pinion, D. The pinion is made solid on the shaft, J. The wheel, A, B, C, is made to

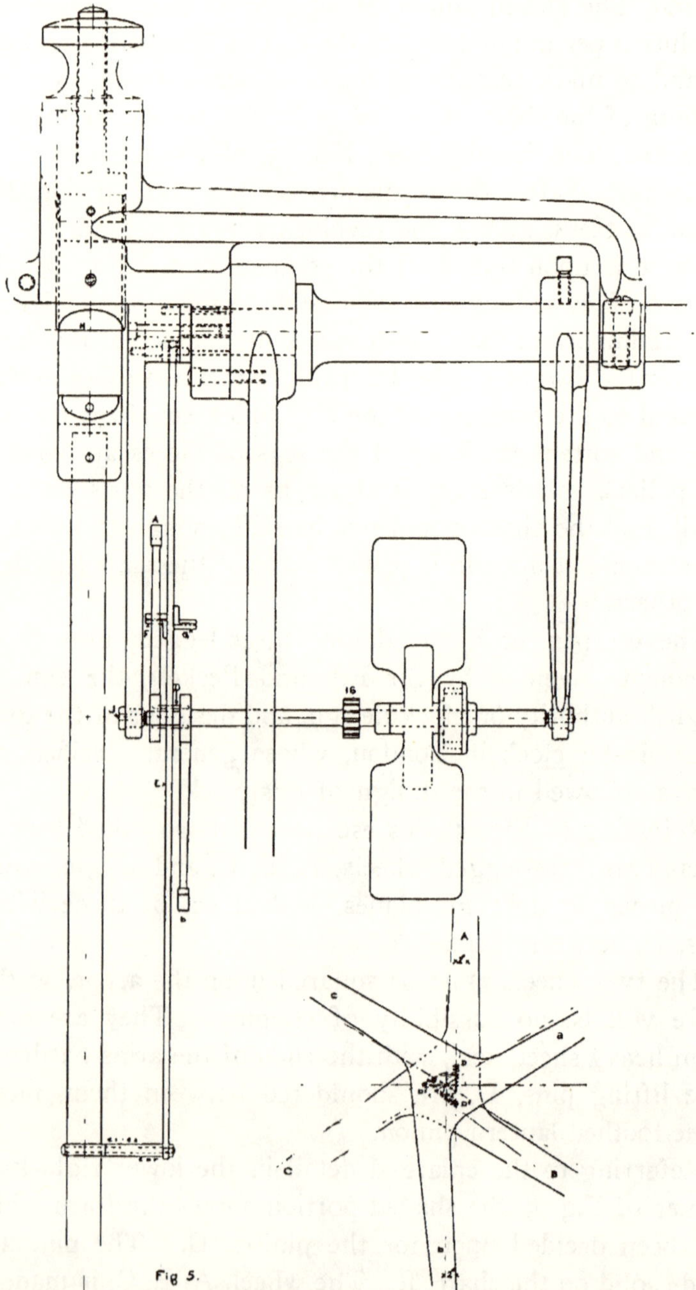

Fig 5.

pass over the pinion, D, and is fitted to a triangular seating the size of the circumscribed triangle of the leaves, D, and against a collar on the shaft. The wheel a, b, c, is fitted to the inscribed triangle of the pinion so that the leaves, D, form the shoulders against which it fits.

The pallets, E and E', also lie in one plane between the wheels, but one stop, F, points forward to receive the A, B, C, teeth and the other, G, backward to receive the a, b, c, teeth, alternately.

The reason for having two wheels is that with one three-legged wheel the pallets could not be far from upright, which would require more dead weight to be moved at every beat in order to have weight enough to give an effective impulse to the pendulum.

There is no particular mechanical advantage in the two wheels being set with the alternate teeth equidistant, appearing like a six-legged wheel. They may be set 90 degrees and 30 degrees to the other set, or at any other angle in order to get a greater inclination of the pallets, if desired. However, the equidistant arrangement is the natural one. I need hardly say that a pair of wheels of this kind is very different from a six-legged wheel, which would move only 30 degrees at each beat, while this moves 60 degrees. There are also other differences.

The distance of the pendulum top, H, or cheeks, from the center of the 'scape wheel, J, equals the diameter of the 'scape wheel.

The lifting pins, D, should not be farther from the center than a thirtieth of this distance; otherwise the pallets, E and E', will have to be inconveniently thin and light. The pins should be so placed that the one which is holding up a pallet and the one which is to lift next, will be vertically over each other, the third being on a level with the center; i. e., they lie in the radii which form the acting faces of the teeth of one of the wheels, Fig. 5.

The fly must be as large as possible, and have a large roller for the spring to act upon.   In the University clock the spring clutch is shown by Fig. 6.

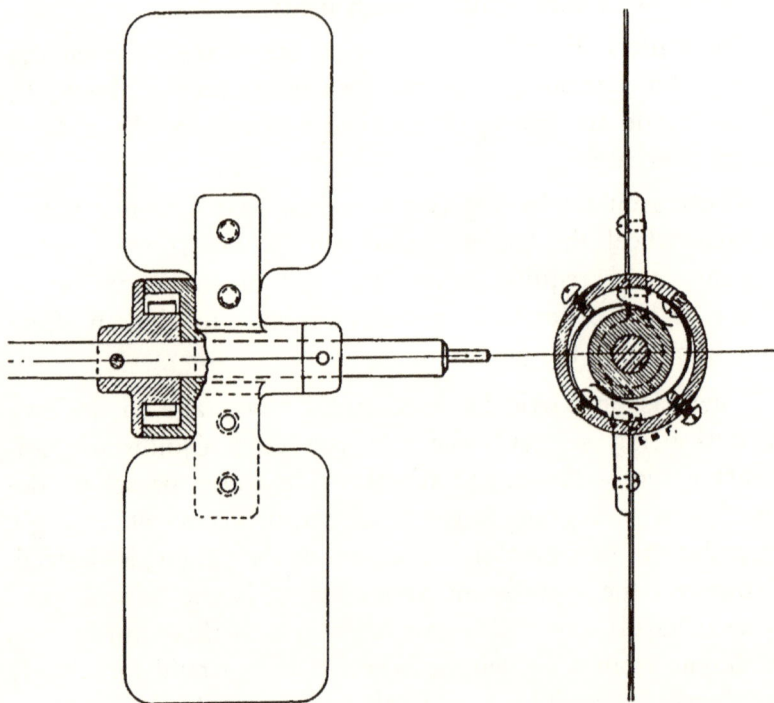

Fig. 6.

The pallet tails, c e', may be bent for the adjustment of the beat.

The beat pins, c', e'2, are tapped into the ends of the pallet tails.   One of them should be threaded left hand, and each has a lock nut on the back.   The outer ends of the pins, where they rest on the pendulum rod, are of ivory, to lessen the chatter; and the one thing which makes a distinction between a gravity and a dead-beat escapement must be avoided, viz.: the beat pins in the gravity escapement must on no account be touched with oil or other grease of

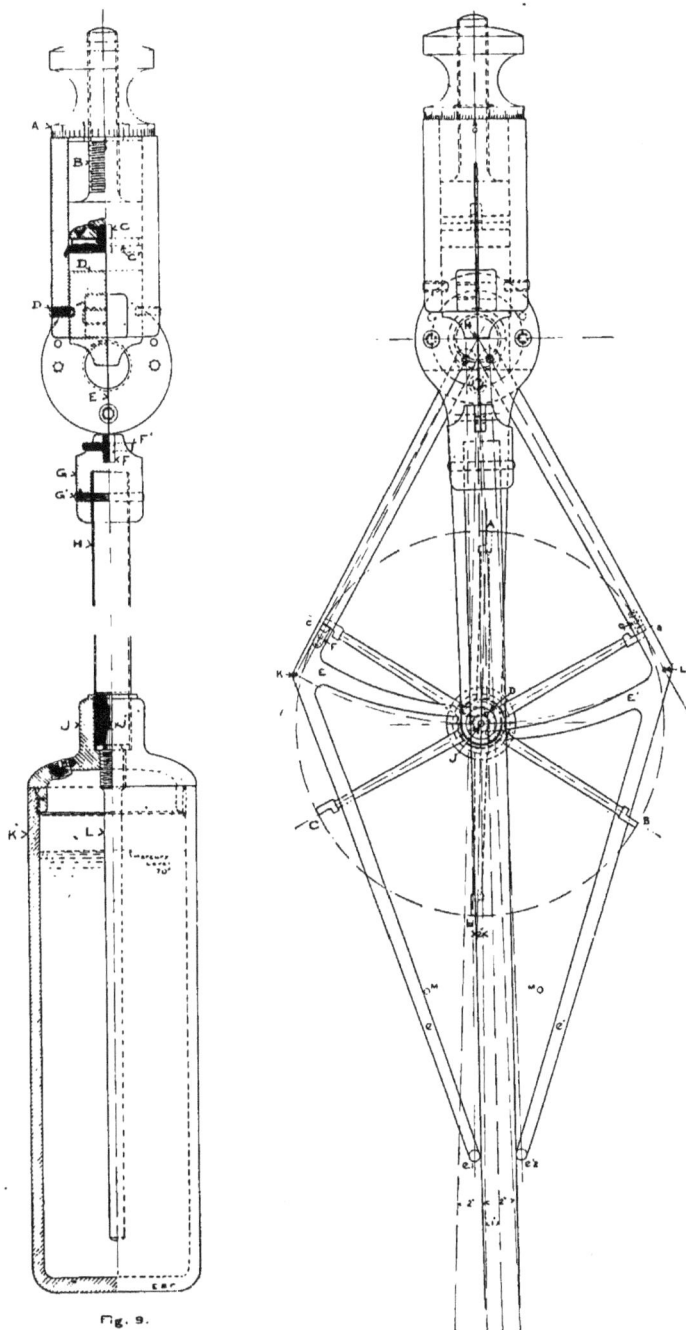

Fig. 9.

any kind, but left absolutely dry, whatever they are made of, because the slightest adhesion between the beat pins and the pendulum rod is fatal to the whole action of the escapement. Care must also be taken that one pallet begins to lift simultaneously with the resting of the other, neither before nor after.

The stops on the pallet arms are of steel and are made as hard as possible, or it would be still better if they were made of agate or other jewels. These stops may have the slightest touch of oil of the best quality, but all surplus must be wiped off.

The distance of the lifting pins, D, from the center, J, should not be more than a fortieth of J, H, or the angle of impulse will be too great to be convenient. It is difficult to make the pallets light enough; the larger the angle of impulse the lighter they must be.

The length of the pallet tails down to the beat pins is a matter of design and appearance, but the action is better with long than with short tails. The length shown in the drawing looks neat, as the two parts are reciprocally parallel, and it is customary to make them in that way.

The pins, D, are placed so that the lifting will take place equally across the line of centers, K, L, as it is then done with the least friction.

Any gravity escapement requires a heavier weight on the going parts than a dead escapement, because it must be strong enough to be sure of lifting the pallets quickly and firmly; but with this form of escapement the superfluous force does not work the pendulum, and it therefore does no harm, if the train is good enough not to waste power in getting over rough places left in cutting the teeth of the wheels. For this reason a high-numbered train is better than a low-numbered one, as these defects are greater on the larger teeth of a low-numbered train; and any defect in this matter will show itself, or rather, make itself heard.

In the gravity escapement, the wheel must have a little

run at the pallets before it begins to lift them, and in order to do this there ought to be two banking pins, M M', for the pallet arms to rest on, just clear of the lifting pins.

The 'scape wheel should be as light as possible, for every blow that is heard in a machine means a loss of power and wear of parts; of course, in an escapement, a sudden stop, and therefore a blow of some amount, is expected, but the light wheel will reduce it to a minimum.

To bring the time train down to plain figures it stands thus: Great wheel, one revolution in six hours, 120 teeth, with a pinion of 20 teeth; hour shaft, 105 teeth, with a pinion of 14 teeth; seven and one-half minute shaft 120 teeth, with a pinion of 15 teeth; one minute shaft, 120 teeth, with a pinion of 12 teeth, giving the 'scape wheel six seconds.

The pendulum, Fig. 9, is suspended from the head or cock shown in the figure, and supported by the clock frame itself, instead of being hung on a wall, since the intention is to set the clock in the center of the clock-room, and also because the weight, forty pounds, is not too much for the clock frame to carry. The head, A, forms a revolving thumb-nut, which is divided into sixty parts around the circumference of its lower edge, and the regulating screw, B, is threaded ten to the inch. A very fine adjustment is thus obtained for regulating the time of the pendulum. The lower end of the regulating screw, B, holds the end of the pendulum spring, E, which is riveted between two pieces of steel, C, and a pin, C', is put through them and the end of the regulating screw, by which to suspend the pendulum.

The cheeks or chops are the pieces D, the lower edges of which form the theoretical point of suspension of the pendulum. These pieces must be perfectly square at their lower edges, otherwise the center of gravity would describe a cylindrical curve. The chops are clamped tightly in place by the setscrews, D', after the pendulum has been hung.

The point of suspension, and therefore the bend of the spring, must be exactly opposite the center of the line of

intersection of the pallet arms, so that there will be no
friction of the beat pins on the pendulum rod.   The lower
end of the regulating screw is grooved on one side, sliding
on a pin to prevent its turning and therefore twisting the
suspension spring when it is raised or lowered.

The spring is about three inches long between its points
of suspension, one and three-eighths inches wide, and one-
sixtieth of an inch thick.   Its lower end is riveted between
two small blocks of steel, F, and suspended from a pin, F',
in the upper end of the cap, G, of the pendulum rod.

The tubular steel portion of the pendulum rod is seven-
eighths of an inch in diameter and one-thirty-second of an
inch thick.   It is enclosed at each end by the solid ends, G
and L, and is made as nearly air tight as possible, in order
to assist in the compensation which is necessary, owing to
changes of temperature and barometer.

The compensation is made by means of mercury inclosed
in a cast-iron bob.   The mercury, the bob and the rod together, weigh forty pounds.   The bob of the pendulum is
a cast-iron jar, K, three inches in diameter inside, one-quarter inch thick at the sides, and five-sixteenths thick at the
bottom, with the cap, J, screwed into its upper end.   The
cap, J, forms also the socket for the lower end of the pendulum rod, H.   The rod, L, one-quarter inch in diameter,
screws into the cap, J, and its large end at the same time
forms a plug for the lower end of the pendulum tube, H.
The pin, J', holds all these parts together.   The rod, L, ex-
tends nearly to the bottom of the jar, and forms a medium
for the transmission of the changes in temperature from the
pendulum tube to the mercury.   The screw in the cap, J, is
for filling or emptying the jar.   The jar is finished as
smoothly as possible, outside and inside, and should be
coated with at least three coats of shellac inside.   Of course
if one was building an astronomical clock, it would be necessary to boil the mercury in the jar in order to drive off the
layer of air between the mercury and the walls of the jar,

but with the smooth finish the shellac will give, in addition to the good work of the machinist, the amount of air held by the jar can be ignored. The cast-iron jar was decided upon because it was safer to handle, can be attached more firmly to the rod with less multiplication of parts, and also on account of the weight as compared with glass, which is the only other thing that should be used, the glass requiring a greater height of jar for equal weight.

Ignoring the rod and its parts for the present, and calling the jar one-third of the weight of the mercury, we shall find that thirty pounds of mercury, at .49 pounds per cubic inch, will fill a cylinder which is three inches inside diameter to a height of 8.816 inches, after deducting for the mass of the rod L, when the temperature of the mercury is 60 degrees F. Mercury expands one-tenth in bulk, while cast-iron expands .0066 in diameter; so the sectional area increases as 1.0066^2, or 1.0132 to 1, therefore the mercury will rise .1-.0132, or .087; then the mercury in our jar will rise .767 of an inch in the ordinary changes of temperature, making a total height of 9.58 inches to provide for; so the jar was made ten inches long.

As this is a one-second pendulum, the length from the point of suspension to the center of gravity, or center of inertia, of the bob, was found by the common equation for the simple pendulum, viz.:

$$t = T \sqrt{\frac{l}{g}}$$

In which t, is one second; T, is 3.1416; l, is the length; and g, is the force of gravity for Chicago.

The force of gravity depends upon the latitude and the elevation above sea level. Barker's Physics, page 105, gives the following approximate formula:

g = 980.6056 — 2.5028 cosine 2, d — .000003 h.

    980.6056 = value of gravity at lat. 45 degrees.

    d = latitude of Chicago = 41 degrees 50 minutes.

h = altitude above sea level, of the clock, in centimeters.

h = 715 x 12 x 2.54.

h = 21793.20 centimeters.

Cosine 2d = Cosine 2 x 41 degrees 50 minutes.

   = Cosine 83 degrees 40 minutes.

   = .1103.

Substituting figures in the formula gives:

g. = 980.6056 — 2.5028 x .1103 — .000003 x 21793.20.

   = 980.6056 — .27605 — .06537

   = 980.2642   dynes.

   = force of gravity at the clock.

Therefore $1 = \dfrac{g}{T^2}$ centimeters.

$= \dfrac{980.2642}{9.8696}$

   = 99.321 centimeters.

   = 39.099134 inches.

Which equals the length of the pendulum rod from its point of suspension to the center of inertia, or center of gravity, on the clock, when it is in a tower 715 feet above sea level, or 135 feet above the mean lake level at Chicago. This is the theoretical length of a mathematical pendulum, but of course the pendulum rod must be stiff enough to avoid the tendency to bend as it receives its impulse from the pallets; and as a bob of forty pounds must be of considerable size, the actual or effective center of the swinging weight will be some small distance below the point given in the formula. This point is called the center of oscillation and also the center of percussion, and is really the point in the bob where a force or blow used to stop the pendulum suddenly would do so without jarring the pendulum in any of its parts or producing any sidewise pressure at its point of suspension. This does not correspond to the center of gravity of the mass of the pendulum, which is a fixed point, but is below it.

Now let us consider some of the forces collected at the center of oscillation.

1—The center of oscillation. If a body oscillate, or swing about a fixed horizontal axis or point of suspension *not* passing through its center of gravity, there is a point in the line drawn from the center of gravity perpendicular to the horizontal axis whose motion is the same as it would be if it were possible to collect the whole mass of the body at that point, and the mass allowed to vibrate, oscillate, or swing as a pendulum about the fixed horizontal axis, or point of suspension. This point is called the *center of oscillation,* and is, as before stated, always *below* the center of gravity. See Fig. 19.

If A be the point of suspension of a body, B, its center of mass, or center of gravity; K equals the length of the radius of gyration of the mass with reference to the point of suspension, A; then there is, in the same straight line with A, B, and on the opposite of B, from A, a point, C, called the *center of oscillation,* which has the following properties:

a—A body may be swung upon A, or at C, indifferently, and in either case it will oscillate pendulum-wise with equal rapidity or in equal time.

b—The body thus suspended at either A, or C, will oscillate at the same rate as an ideal simple pendulum of the length A, C.

c—This body will, if struck at C, oscillate round A, without producing any pressure on the point of suspension or supporting axis A.

d—Though the support at A were withdrawn. as, for instance, if the body were floating submerged in water, and, if the body were at rest, all that part of the body above A, would move in a direction opposite to that in which C is struck. For every point C, at which a body may be struck, or every *center of percussion,* there is a corresponding point A, on the other side of the center of the figure through which passes an axis of spontaneous rotation round which the body rotates; i. e., if the lower part is suddenly pulled forward, the upper part above A, will move backward.

e—The distance, A, C, is equal to $\dfrac{k^2}{AB}$ when the body is suspended at A, k being the radius of gyration in this case; or, $\frac{k_1^2}{CB}$ when suspended at C. k being the radius of gyration in this case. The radii of gyration are so related that $\frac{k^2}{AB} = \frac{k_1^2}{CB}$

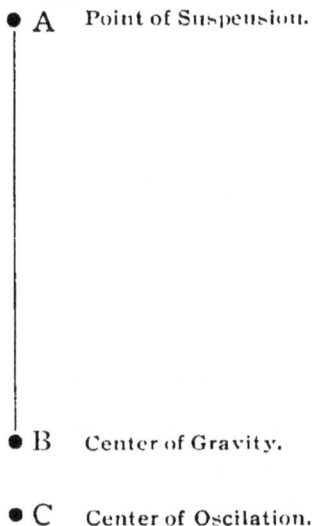

● A   Point of Suspension.

● B   Center of Gravity.

● C   Center of Oscilation.

Fig. 19. Principal Points of a Simple Pendulum.

2—The *radius* of *oscillation* is the distance of the *center* of *oscillation* from the point of suspension; see Fig. 19. and equals the square of the *radius* of *gyration* divided by the distance of the center of gravity from the point of suspension or axis.

3—The *center* of *gyration* with reference to an axis, is a point at which, if it were possible to collect the entire *weight* of a body at one point, its *moment* of *inertia* will remain unchanged; or, in a revolving body, the point at which the whole weight of the body may be concentrated. The distance of this point from the axis or point of suspension is the *radius* of *gyration*.

4—The *moment* of *inertia* of the *weight* of a body with respect to an axis, or point of suspension, is the algebraic *sum* of the products obtained by multiplying the weight of each elementary particle by the square of its distance from the axis, or point of suspension. If the moment of inertia with respect to an axis equal I, the weight of any element of the body equal w, and its distance from the axis equal r, we have $I = \Sigma\,(wr^2)$.

The moment of inertia varies in the same body according to the position of the axis. It is the least possible when the axis passes through the center of gravity. To find the moment of inertia of the body referred to a given axis, divide the body into small parts of regular figure.

Multiply the weight of each part by the square of the distance of its center of gravity from the axis. The sum of the products is the moment of inertia.

The value of the moment of inertia thus obtained will be more nearly exact, the smaller and more numerous the parts into which the body is divided.

The moments of inertia of regular solids, the formulae for which apply to our problem, are as follows:

a—Rod or bar of uniform thickness, with respect to an axis perpendicular to the length of the rod:
$$I = W\,(\tfrac{1}{3}l^2 + d^2)$$
.W = weight of rod. 2l = length of rod. d = distance of center of gravity from the axis of suspension.

b—Thin circular plate with its axis on its own plane:
$$I = W\,(\frac{r^2}{4} + d^2)$$
r = radius of plate.

c—Circular ring, axis perpendicular to its own plane:
$$I = W\,(\frac{R^2 \times r^2}{2} + d^2)$$
R and r equals exterior and interior radii of the ring.

The *moment* of *inertia* $\Sigma\,wr^2$ numerically, equals the *weight* of a body, which, if concentrated at the distance *unity* from the axis of rotation, or suspension, would require the same work to produce a given increase in angular velocity that the actual body requires.

5—The *center* and *radius* of *gyration*. The center of gyration with reference to an axis of suspension, is a point at which, if the entire weight of a body be concentrated, its moment of inertia will remain unchanged. The distance of the point from the axis, or point of suspension, is the *radius* of *gyration*.

If W equals the weight of a body, I equals $\gtrless wr^2$ or its moment of inertia, and k equals its radius of gyration.

$$\text{Then I} = Wk^2 = \gtrless wr^2$$

$$k = \sqrt{\frac{\gtrless wr^2}{W}}$$

That is: the moment of inertia equals the weight multiplied by the square of the radius of gyration.

To find the radius of gyration, divide the body into a considerable number of small parts, the greater the number of parts, the more accurate the result, then take the mean of all the squares of the distances of the parts from the axis, or point of suspension, and find the square root of the mean square. Or, if the moment of inertia is known, divide it by the weight and extract the square root.

The principal radii of gyration called for in the consideration of this pendulum are as follows:

a. Rod, axis perpendicular to its length $= k = l\sqrt{\dfrac{l}{3}}$

b. Circular plate axis in its own plane, $= k = \dfrac{r}{2}$

c. Circular ring, its axis perpendicular to the plane of the ring.

$$k = \sqrt{\frac{R^2 + r^2}{2}}$$

The value of k, and of the squares of the radii of gyration, for the above formulae are:

Radius of gyration.	Squares of the radii of gyration.
a. .57731	$\dfrac{l}{3}$ l^2
b. .7071	$\dfrac{l}{2}$ r^2
c. .7071 $\sqrt{R^2 + r^2}$	$(R^2 + r^2) \div 2$

6—*Center* of *Percussion*, of a body oscillating about a fixed axis, is the point at which, if a blow is struck by the body, the percussive action is the same as though the whole mass of the body were concentrated at that point; see also paragraph No. c and d in the definition of centers of oscillation. The center of percussion is identical with the center of oscillation. All of us who are familiar with the use of the baseball bat will have some very vivid remembrances of the same percussive action. When the bat is struck above the center of percussion, do you remember how it made your fingers tingle, and when it hit too low down, how the bat went waltzing off toward the field?

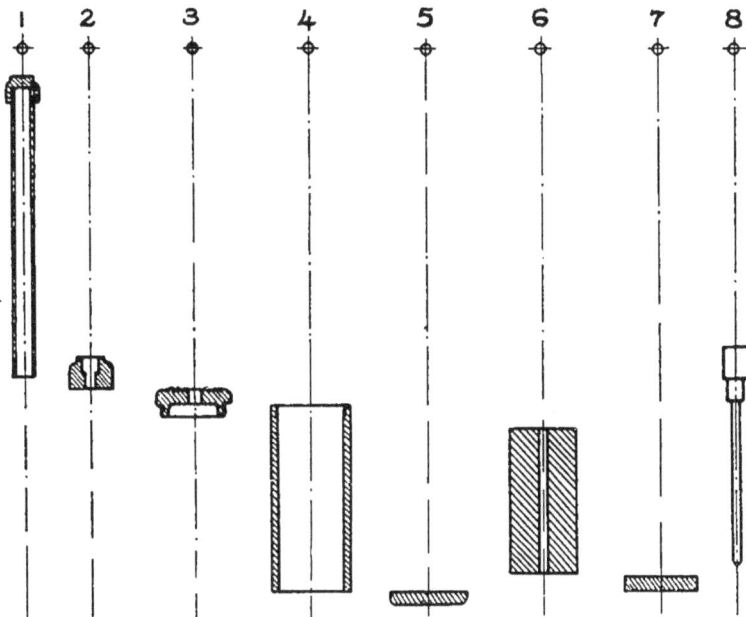

Fig. 20. Parts of pendulum as separated for calculating the weight.

Fig. 20 shows in table form the subdivisions of the pendulum and the results of the application of the formulae, from which we get the following results:

*Squares of Radii of Gyration.....	1	2	3	4	5
	.119140	.30664	1.5312	2.6562	1.422988
†Weights of Parts	1.2c6036	.271625	.939497	6.480522	.728
Moments of Inertia	.143686	.083291	1.438562	17.213504	1 035944
§Center of Oscill'n	.0304	.00784	.03916	.06970	.03630

*Squares of Radii of Gyration.....	6	7	8	Total.
	1 137573	1.125	3.675	
†Weights of Parts	27.5c0956	2.597710	.401	40.125356
Moments of Inertia	31.285c23	2.922412	14.736750	68 859172
§Centres of Oscil'n	.02830	.02870	.93992	1.17082

*The square root of the mean square equals .9448, which, according to the formula, equals the distance from B to C, Fig. 19 by this formula.

†Then, by the formula, we want the square root of 68.859 divided by 40.125 (the weight) equals 1.31009, which is the distance between B and C, by this formula.

§By the formula 1.17082 is the distance from B to C.

Now here are three different results by three formulæ; theoretically they should agree, but I have not succeeded in finding any one who can make them do so; I find also, that all the eminent authorities give as a final conclusion the fact that it is, after all, still a matter of experiment and trial; so I do not think we need to worry ourselves over the lack of a definite result.

After all the calculations are made, there still remains the effect of barometric changes which are not included in the formulæ given.

Prof. S. W. Stratton, of the U. S. Bureau of Standards at Washington, tells me of a new nickel steel alloy known by the name of "Invar," made in France by the Societè de Commentry-Fourchambault, d'Imphy. The coefficient of expansion of this alloy is practically zero, and is to be used in some of the new apparatus where it is desirable to eliminate temperature effects. This new metal will be the ideal material for pendulums.

We will now go back to the hour shaft and proceed towards the dials. The pair of beveled gears of 44 and 48 teeth, with their shafts at 90 degrees, are for leading off to the large dials, which should be above the clock. It is best to use the well-known universal joint, see Fig. 7, to connect the shaft which goes from this pair of gears to the nest of gears, Fig. 8, which will run the hands on the four dials; and as the four gears receiving the impulse from the hour shaft must have the same speed as the hour shaft, they must all have the same diameter, and the one on the vertical shaft in the center must be enough larger in diameter to run the hour gears without their interference with each other. The number of teeth in the gears of the nest of four is 44, and the driving wheel is 48, giving center angles of 42 degrees 30 minutes for the 44 toothed wheel, and 47 degrees 30 minutes for the 48-toothed wheel. The universal-jointed shafts from the clock to the nest of gears, and those from this nest of gears to the back of the dials must have the slip, or expansion joint, shown in Fig. 7, to allow for all expansion caused by changes in the weather, wind pressure on the dials, etc.

The shafts to the dials will, of course, revolve once an hour, and so these shafts carry the minute hands. To obtain the motion of the hour hand the usual combinations of wheels of 96 teeth and pinions of 24 teeth, driving wheels of 90 teeth and pinions of 30 teeth, are used behind each dial, to obtain one revolution in 12 hours. Of course, any other combination would do equally well, so long as it satis-

fies the condition of the following equation: $\dfrac{W\,W^1}{P\,P^1} = 12$

W equals teeth in the wheels; P equals those in the pinion.

In case the hour shaft of the clock is not perpendicularly under the nest of gears above, care must be taken that a short section of the universal-jointed shaft at each end *is*

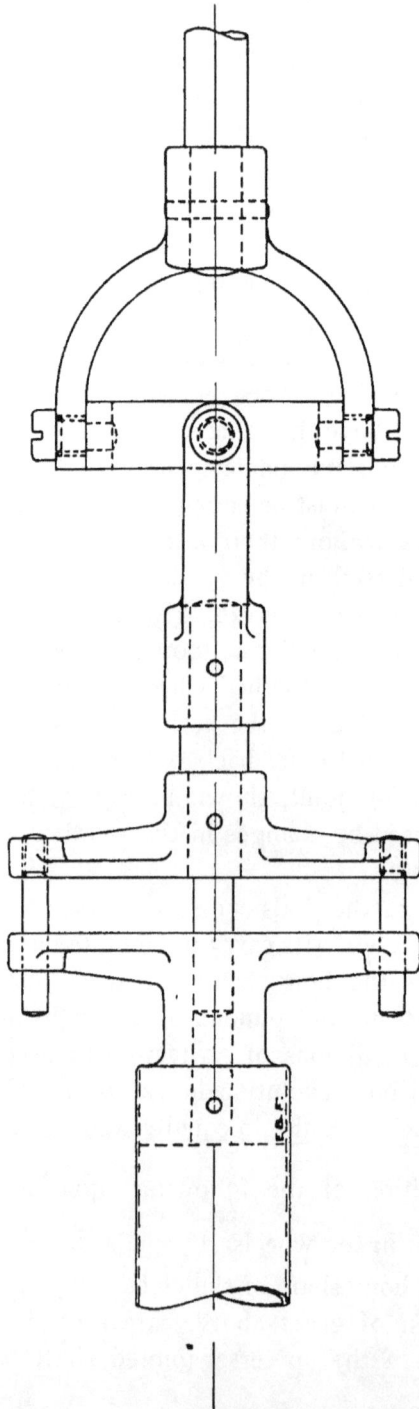

Fig. 7.

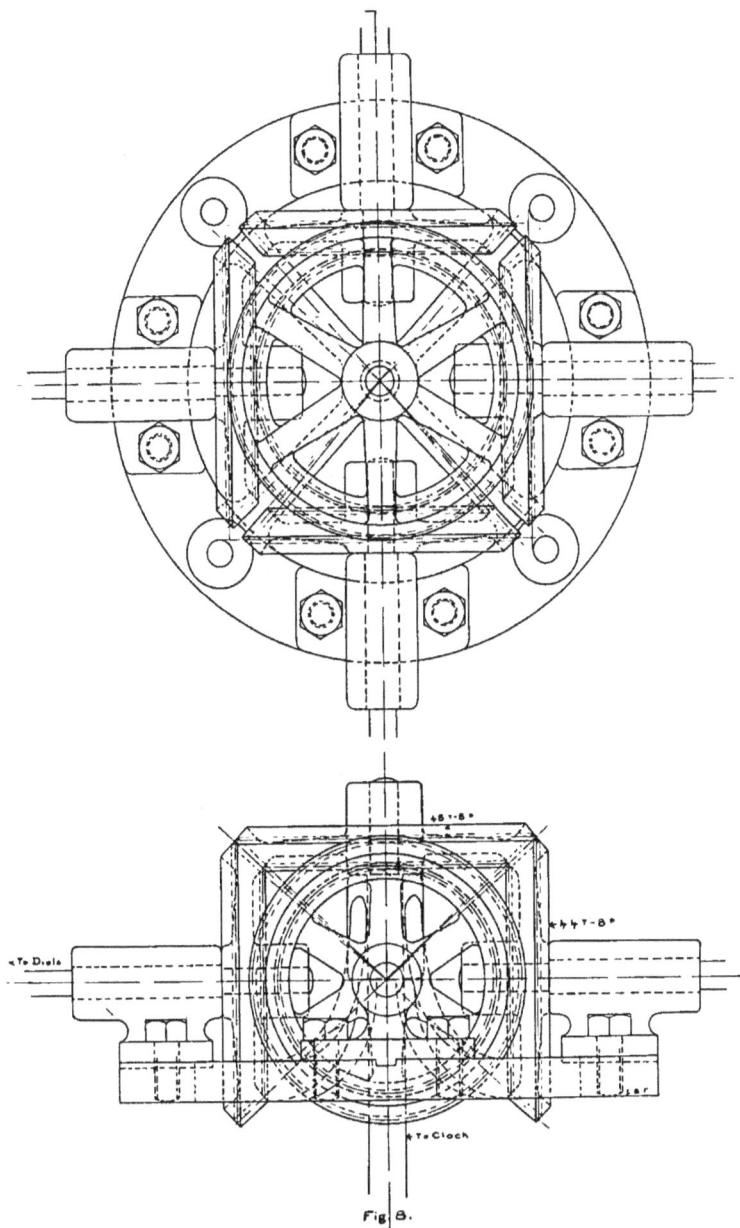

Fig 8.

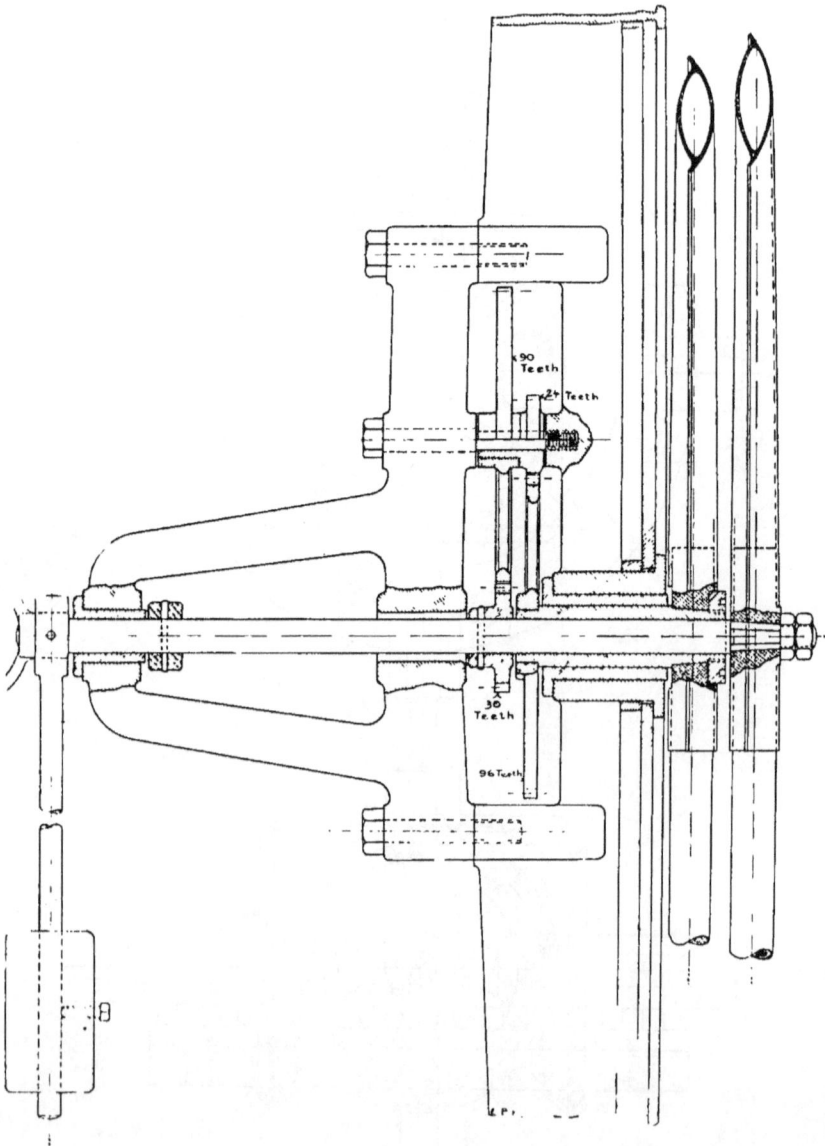

Fig. 17. Arrangement of Hands, Counter Balances and Hour and Minute
Wheels at the Centers of the Clock Dials.

exactly perpendicular, in order to avoid the loss of motion, and therefore of regularity of time, which will occur if the angles of obliquity are not equal.

The hands are made of copper, elliptical in section, being made up of two circular segments brazed together at the edges, with internal diaphragms to stiffen them. The minute hand is straight and perfectly plain, with a blunt point.

At the center of the dial the width of the minute hand is one-thirteenth of its length, tapering to about half as much at the point.

The hour hand is about the same width, ending just short of the dial figure and terminating in a palm or ornament. The external counterpoises are one-third the length of the minute hand, and of such a shape that they will not be confounded with either of the hands; a cylinder, painted the same color as the dial, makes a good counterpoise. This counterpoise may be partly on the inside of the dial if it is desired to keep it invisible, but it should not be omitted, as it saves a good deal of power, prevents the twisting of the arbors, and also assists in overcoming the action of the wind on the hands. Two-thirds of the counterpoise weight may be inside.

The diameter of the dials and the weight of the bells are the two most important factors in the design of a clock.

This clock was designed, as the specifications show, for four dials of 12 feet diameter and an hour bell of 7,000 pounds. As it is not yet known in what tower the University will set the clock, and therefore the height of the dials above the ground, the mechanical parts are designed for a 15 foot dial.

The diameter of the dials should not be less than one-tenth of their height above the ground, so the limit of height for a 15-foot dial should be 150 feet.

The figures and minutes together will take up one-third of the radius of the dial; the figures two-thirds of this, or two-ninths of the radius, and the minutes two-thirds of

the remaining one-ninth of the radius, with every fifth minute more strongly marked than the rest.

How many of the thousands of people who pass daily
up and down Michigan avenue, do you suppose have ever
noticed, or if they have noticed it once, have ever thought
of it again, that the clock face on the Kimball Company's
tower has the name of the company instead of the numbers,
to indicate the hours? In several towns in New England
I have seen the words Memorial Gift distributed round the
dial, and in one case the name of the giver was used for the
same purpose. In Toronto, Canada, I passed the big 22
foot dial on the City Hall clock fully 25 times before I
noticed that there were no figures or letters of any kind but
only 12 broad flat surfaces about the width of the figure
three of the Roman numerals, as used on clock dials, and
I find that Sir Edmund Beckett specially recommends the
last form for illuminated dials, as there can be a greater
area of lighted surface in the figure ring, which will add
to the facility in reading the time. If you will stop to
think, you will see at once that it is never the *figures* that
you read, but the *angles* of the minute and hour hands in
their relation to each other and to the 12 sub-divisions of
the dial; therefore on this clock the hours will be indicated
by heavy bars or bands, about five inches wide, instead of
by the numerals.

The dial proper will be illuminated and is therefore built
up in segments; the outer series containing the minutes and
hours, in six segments; the inner series of four segments
making up the center of the dial.

The frame is of cast-iron, made in such sections that the
opal glass, of about 22 ounces per square foot, can be set
in it, as in ordinary sash, the segments being made to fit
together with the lap or tongue and groove joints, so as to
exclude the rain and snow.

The hands and figures will be painted black, and the
frame work of the dial gilded. A space of about three feet

at the back of each dial will be enclosed and this wall will be used to support the illuminating medium, which in this case will probably be about 60 incandescent lamps to each dial, with powerful reflectors that will distribute their light as evenly as possible over the whole surface of the dial.

THE STRIKING TRAIN.

As the striking part should be wound up every 24 hours, with an allowance of six hours extra for carelessness about the time of winding, provision must be made for 30 hours' work. There are 156 strokes in 24 hours, and allowing 60 strokes extra for overtime, makes 216 strokes to provide for.

The train is arranged to allow the second wheel, No. 32, one revolution for each stroke on the bell. The cam, No. 27, on the going shaft has 12 parts, therefore it will have one-twelfth revolution to each stroke.

If we allow 18 teeth on the pinion, No. 31, on the second shaft, No. 30, the great wheel, No. 29, will have 216 teeth, or one revolution for every 12 strokes, which gives 18 turns in 30 hours. The length of the winding barrel, No. 26, must of course, provide for this.

The bell, of 7,000 pounds, calls for a striking weight of one-fiftieth of its weight, or 140 pounds. The levers, Nos. 28 and 28', are in the proportion of one to three, giving a pressure on the cam surfaces, No. 27, of 420 pounds, and adding one-tenth for friction, makes it equal to 480, or for safety, 500 pounds pressure on the cams, which are of cast-steel. The end of the lever, No. 28, has a hardened steel shoe to reduce the friction to its lowest point.

The second wheel, No. 32, has 120 teeth, with a pinion of 20 teeth, No. 33, on the third shaft, giving six revolutions of the fly shaft and therefore of the fly.

The details of the fly and its clutch are shown in Fig. 10. The vanes are so made that they may be set to present any desired amount of surface to the air. This gives us an opportunity to determine definitely the striking periods,

(38)

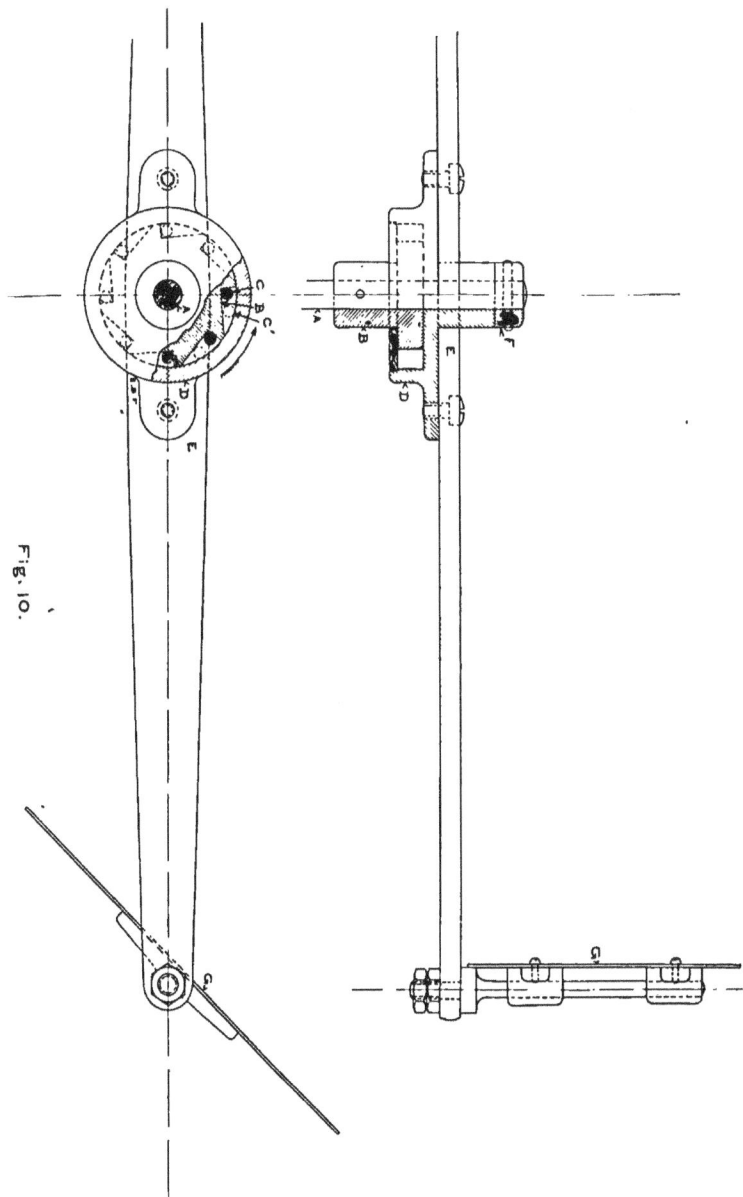

Fig. 10.

which on a bell of 7,000 pounds should be very slow, as it
requires two or two and one-half seconds for each stroke in
order to obtain the full vibration of the bell.

The fly clutch is the familiar roller clutch, and is made
with a set of eight steel cylinders, C, rolling in angular
spaces, B. As the shaft starts to revolve, one or more of
these rollers is always in position to roll into the angle
between the ratchet wheel, B, and its case, D, and so start
the vanes. As the shaft stops its revolution, the vanes, G,
and the case, D, are free to revolve, so that, by their momentum they roll the cylinders out of the acute angles and
into the right angled spaces, which are large enough to
hold the rollers free of all moving parts.

The locking plate, No. 39, Fig. 1, is carried forward by
a wheel, No. 38, of 78 teeth, which equals the number of
strokes in 12 hours. This is moved one tooth for each
stroke, by the pinion, No. 37, of 12 teeth, on the going
shaft, No. 25.

The going shaft has a winding gear of 96 teeth, with a
pinion on the winding shaft of 24 teeth. This pinion slides
on a feather so that it can be thrown out of gear after
winding, in order to save power.

Fig. 11 shows the positions, in full lines, of the various
parts of the locking plate work of the striking side at seven
and one-half minutes of the striking of the hour, except
the cam or snail, j, which is shown at the instant after the
striking begins. The total angular movement of the hour
pin from the point of first contact to the warning is 22½
degrees.

The movement is as follows: The hour pin, a, in wheel
No. 9, moving in the direction of the arrow, begins to de-
press the lever, b, on the shaft, c, this raises the levers, d
and e. The lever, d, carries the roller, d', and e, carries
the pin, e'. The pin, f, drops into notches, h, on the locking plate, No. 39. After an angular movement of 22½
degrees, the hour pin has raised the roller, d', and the pin,

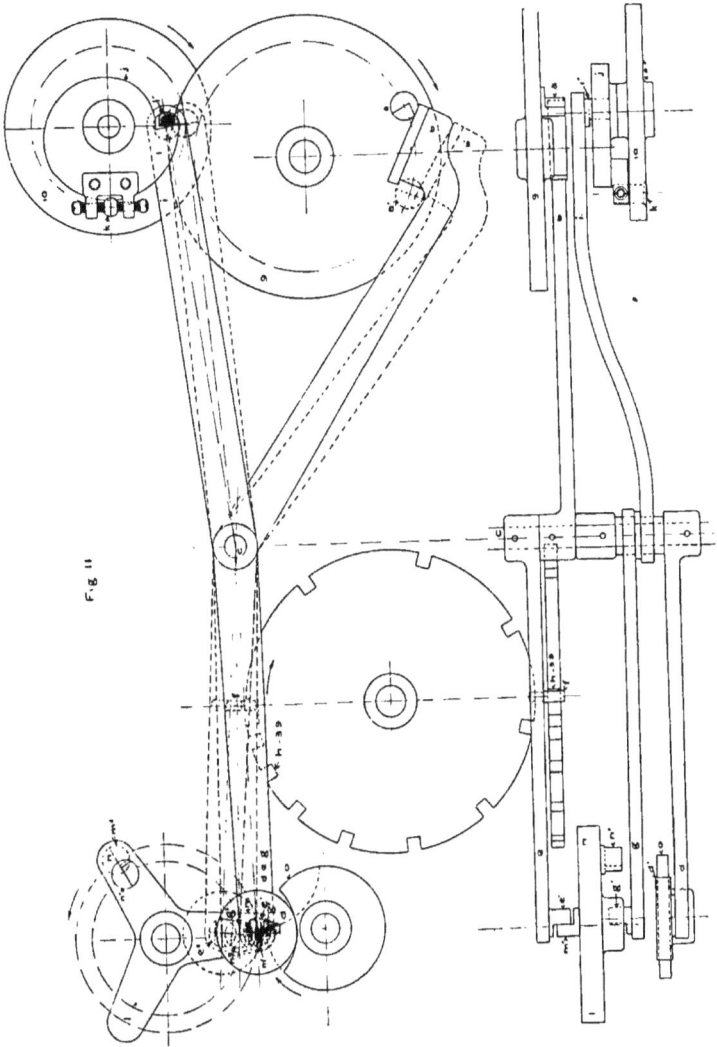

Fig. 11

e', to d" e", when the pin, m', will pass at five minutes of the
hour, allowing the fly to revolve 240 degrees, giving the
warning and revolving the cam, o, 22½ degrees, or far
enough for the roller, d', to rest on its circumference, there-
by preventing f, from dropping back into the notch, h. As
the pin, m', passes, n', will come in contact with the pin,
g', in the lever, g. The lever, g, receives its impulse from
the snail or cam, j, on the wheel, No. 10, which revolves
once in 15 minutes. The cam is so designed that the pin,
g', comes up into position six minutes before the hour, and
so catches pin, n', as it comes along at five minutes of the
hour. The pin, i', drops a sufficient interval before the
hour (about three seconds), for the striking mechanism to
get in motion so as to give the first blow of the hour exactly on the first second of the hour. The set screws shown
at K, allow an angular movement of five seconds either way
to give the required adjustment.

After the pin, g', has released n', of course the fly revolves
until the required number of strokes have been given; the
pin, f, dropping upon the locking plate for each blow, until
one of the notches comes under it, when, f, drops into it,
letting the roller, d', drop into the hollow in the cam, o, and
the lever, e, drop, so that the pin, e', catches m', when all
movement ceases except the fly, which, released by the
clutch, continues to revolve until its momentum has been
overcome.

Of course the movements of the snail, j, and of the parts
that work with it are repeated every 15 minutes; but as the
pin, n', is not in position, there is no movement of the rest
of the hour-striking train.

The train must be so adjusted that after striking the
hour the hammer shall be left at the top of its lift, and
ready for the next blow, though I think it would be better
to leave it at about three-quarters lift, so that there would
be less strain on the points of the faces of the cams of the
hour-striking wheel. The cam faces of this wheel are gen-
erated in the same manner as for the chime side, see Fig. 13.

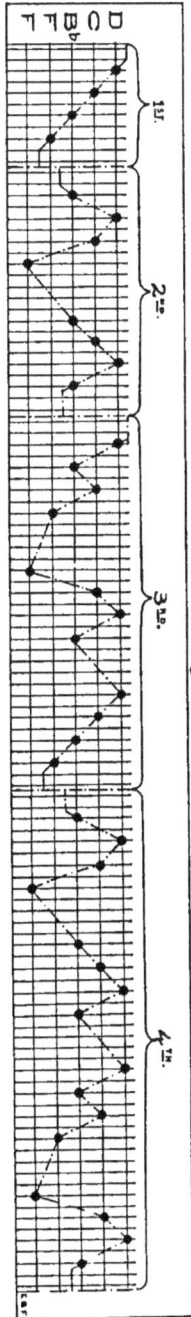

Fig. 12.

THE CHIME TRAIN.

The Westminster Chime, so-called, which is a copy of the chime of St. Mary's at Cambridge, England, and which originated over 100 years ago, has been adopted for the quarters in this clock. The notes are E, D, C, and G; or, as arranged by the Meneely Company; F on a bell of 2,079 pounds; B flat 875 pounds; C, 616 pounds; D, 437 pounds, and with the hour bell to give the note B flat an octave below. If we give the numbers 6, 3, 2, 1, to the chime, the arrangement of the chime is as follows:

Second Quarter $\left\{ \begin{array}{l} 3126 \\ 3213 \\ 1326 \\ 6213 \\ 1236 \end{array} \right.$

$\left. \begin{array}{l} 3126 \\ 3213 \\ 1326 \end{array} \right\}$ Fourth Quarter

Third Quarter

$\left. \begin{array}{l} 6213 \\ 1236 \end{array} \right\}$ First Quarter

If you study this table carefully, you will see that the chimes are repeated twice in an hour. The cams are arranged to turn once every hour.

The interval between the sets of strokes is of considerable importance, in order to enable the listener to read the quarters correctly. Taking the interval between the strokes of each set of four strokes as a standard, Sir Edmund Beckett found that two and one-half spaces or intervals between the sets of four strokes gave the best result. Now to avoid the fractions, and calling the spaces two, then there will be five spaces between sets, or 55 spaces, and as the chime is repeated twice in the hour, this would give 110 spaces on the cam surfaces for each hour. The chime laid out graphically would look like Fig. 12, which explains itself. As F is struck by two cams, it has been given two lines.

Allowing two teeth on the great wheel, No. 54, for each space will make 220 teeth on the great wheel, which, with a pinion, No. 55, of 22 teeth, gives 10 revolutions of the second shaft, No. 56, and one revolution to each set of four strokes in the chime. On the second shaft is a wheel, No. 57, of 120 teeth, driving a pinion, No. 58, of 20 teeth on the fly shaft, thus giving six revolutions to each set of four strokes in the chime. The fly clutch and other parts are the same as in the striking side. There are five cams; the first will strike all of the No. 1 bells at the proper intervals; the second all of the No. 2 bells; the third all of the No. 3 bells, while the fourth and fifth will divide the number six strokes between them. This is necessary because there are two periods when the No. 6 bells come so near together that it would be impossible to get the levers raised in time for the second stroke.

The striking weights on these bells increase from one-sixtieth to one-fortieth of the weight of the bells, from the large to the small ones, so that F, bell will have a striking weight of 35 pounds; B flat, of 18 pounds; C, of 12 pounds and D, of 11 pounds. As there are two F hammers, the total weight of the hammers is 111 pounds. Of course we can make the pressure on the cam surfaces anything we please, by altering the relative length of the arms of the respective levers. There cannot be more than three of the six levers on the cams at the same time, as you will observe by referring to the assembled drawing, Fig. 1, so that the greatest possible weight would be that covered by raising the three largest hammers, or 88 pounds.

The parts have been proportioned to use, as nearly as possible, the same driving power as on the striking side.

The main driving shaft also carries the locking plate, t', divided properly for the four quarters.

In the locking plate work of the chime side, the wheel, No. 9, Fig. 14, on the hour shaft of the time train carries the pins a^1, a^2, a^3, a^4, which depresses lever, b, and raises levers, c, d, and e, allowing the pin, m', to pass c', raising e, out of slot e', in the locking plate, t', and the roller, d', out of the cam, o, allowing the fly and the three armed lever, k, l, m, to revolve 240 degrees, when the pin, l', is

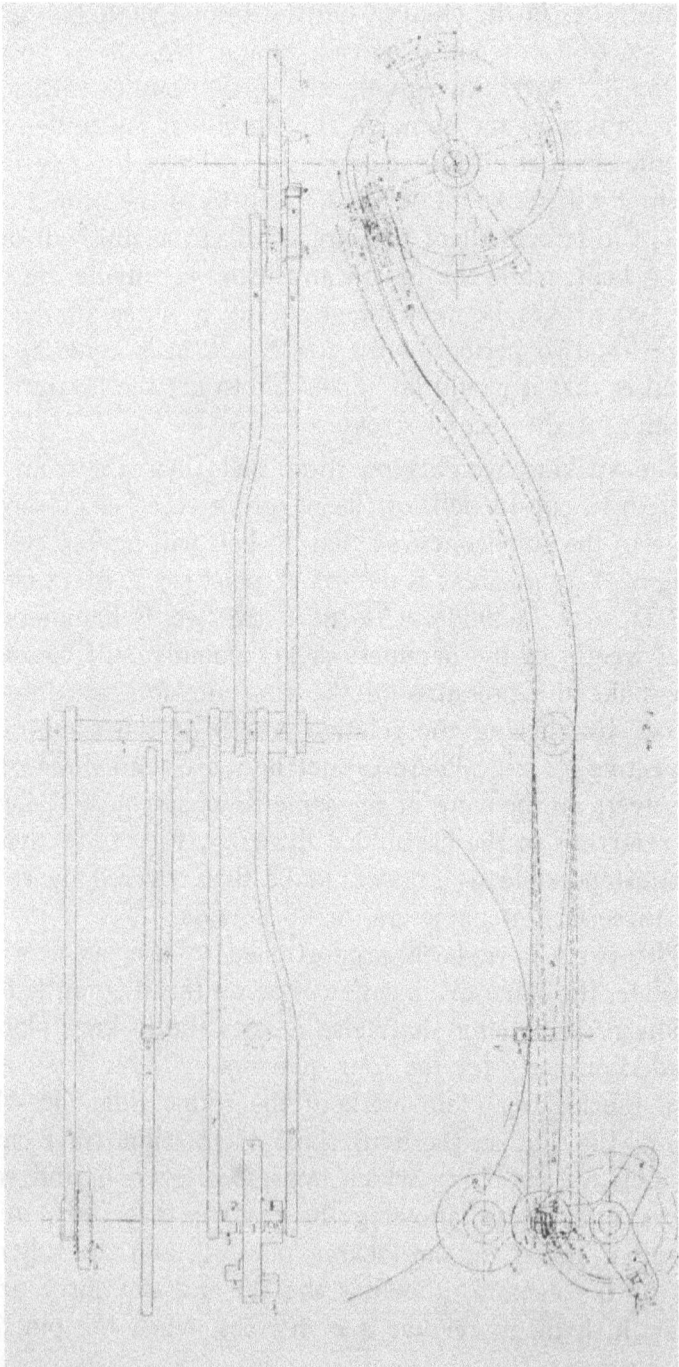

caught by pin, h′, on the lever, h, which has, in the meantime, been raised up to its position by the pin, g′, in the lever, g, riding on the cam surfaces, f¹, f², f³, f⁴, on the rim of the wheel, No. 9.

The pin, g′, drops from these cams allowing pin, l′, to pass, when the ringing of the quarters proceeds, and closes, the same as in the striking of the hours.

The cams, f, are faced with hardened steel, and f¹, f² and f³, are set so that they will discharge the quarters at such an interval before the end of the quarter, that they will strike the first blow on the first second of the next quarter. f⁴, is made to drop the pin, g′, at such a period before the end of the hour that the interval between the last stroke of the fourth quarter chime will be one second more than that between the parts of the chime. If you will refer to the graphic form of the chime, Fig. 12, you will see that the interval between the sets of four strokes is five, and the interval between strokes is two. Allowing two seconds between strokes of the chime, to obtain the full volume of sound, five seconds between sets, and six seconds at the end, we shall have 45 seconds of time, or an angular movement of four and five-tenths degrees ahead of the quarters. In order to obtain exact time at this point the cam face f⁴ is made adjustable.

A cam as used here is a tooth which is to raise a lever to its limit without assistance, while a tooth in a wheel would be assisted by the one behind it; and as the greatest strain comes when the cam is getting the lever started from a standstill, the cam must be so formed as to begin the lift at the end of the lever where the greatest power is required, and the extreme end of the lever must be carried up to the exact moment of dropping, and then let drop suddenly at that exact moment.

Of course the theoretical curve of the cam surfaces should be the epicycloid; but this construction by means of arcs of circles is just as good in actual practice, if designed for

Fig. 13.

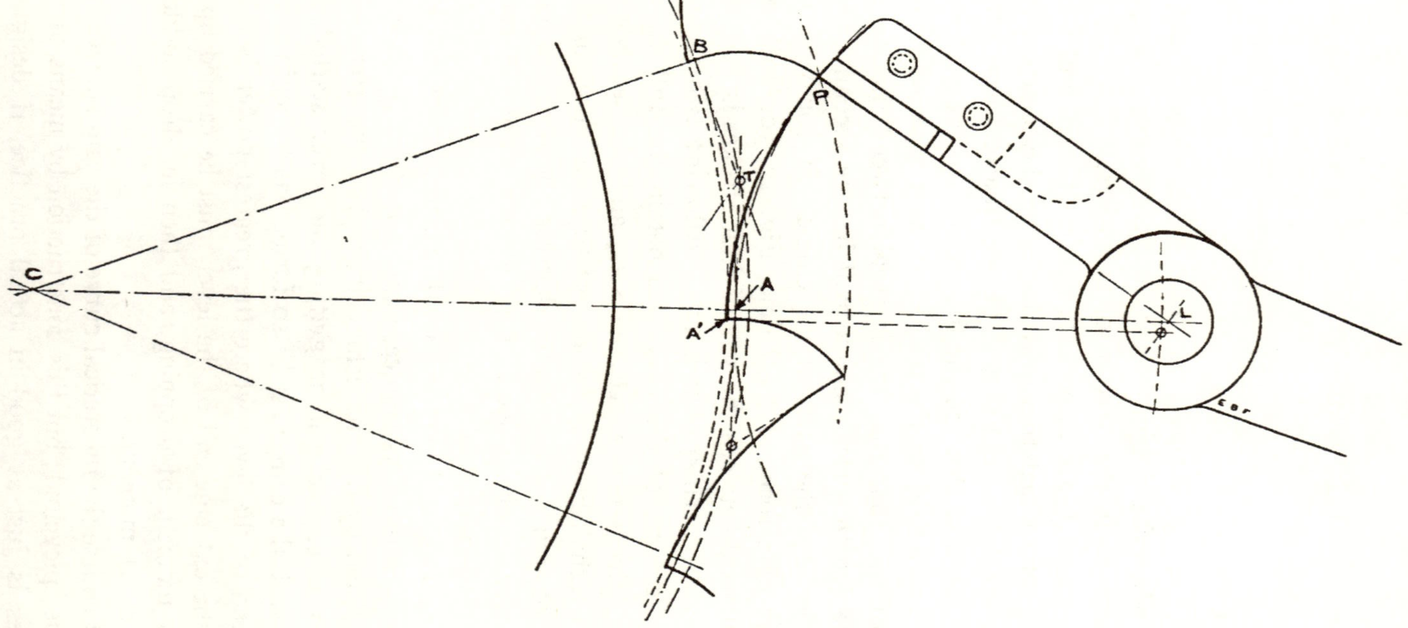

each cam separately. By reference to Fig. 13, C, A, L, is the line of centers; L, the lever center; A, is the pitch circle of the cam; A', B, is the pitch distance, which equals A B, plus one-eighth, for clearance as the lever drops, so that it will not strike the cam below. A, P, is the arc of the lever. Draw A, T, tangent to the pitch circle at A, and B, T, tangent to the pitch circle at B. From P, draw a tangent to the lever arc, and the intersection of these three tangents will be the center of an arc of a circle which will be the proper curve for the cam surface, to carry the end of the lever at the beginning and end of its service. The cams must be backed off for clearance as the lever falls.

THE SHAPES AND WEIGHTS OF BELLS.

Of course we are not concerned with the bells that are to be used with this clock, as they are to be supplied by the University. But the fact remains that, as the size of the clock depends, for one of its factors, upon the size of the bell, it will be necessary for us to know something of the proper proportions and method of obtaining the full vibration and tone, from any given bell, or series of bells. The theory of the design of bells to produce a given series of notes, is based upon the law, that the number of vibrations in a second, in *similar* bells—that is, bells whose variations in proportion are alike—varies as the square of the thickness, divided by the diameter; or, the depth of the notes, or the time of vibration varies as the diameter, divided by the square of the thickness. So if we wanted to make a set of bells of the *same* thickness, not *proportionate* thickness, their other dimension must be as the square roots of a set of numbers in the *inverse ratio* of the vibrations belonging to the proposed notes. But if the thickness itself varies as the diameter, the sizes will vary simply as those numbers vary; and therefore, all of the dimensions of a peal of eight bells will be in the proportions:

$$1, \quad \tfrac{8}{9}, \quad \tfrac{4}{5}, \quad \tfrac{3}{4}, \quad \tfrac{2}{3}, \quad \tfrac{3}{5}, \quad \quad \tfrac{1}{2},$$

or, 60″, 53 1-3″, 48″, 45″, 40″, 36″, 32″, 30″.
This being the diameter in inches of a peal of eight bells in the key of D flat.

The weights of *similar* bells vary as the cubes of their diameters; therefore the weights of a peal of eight bells would be, with the tenor weighing 100 for facility of comparison:

100, —70.23, —51.2, —42.2, —29.63, —21.6, —15.18, —12.5
But the question at once arises, what is the proper weight
for a given note or a given size? Taking 6 feet diameter
as a convenient standard, the *least* weight for a bell of 72
inches would be 8,064 pounds. Such a bell will be very
near B flat according to the universal pitch, in which A
has 880 vibrations per second, or, that number multiplied
or divided by some power of 2. The diameter of bells on
that scale is about 13 times the thickness of the sound bow.

The sound bow should not be thinner than this, for there
is a fullness and softness about a thick bell which a thin one
can never have, and this loss of tone is even greater now,
than it was a hundred years ago on account of the quality of
the copper used in the bell.

The modern process of smelting gives copper that is less
tough and will hold less tin without becoming brittle, as
well as being apparently incapable of a certain softness of
tone which the old bells sometimes have, and which is very
seldom secured in the modern ones.

Sir Edmund Beckett says: "After trying and observing
the effect of a great many patterns, and without favoring
any particular curve, the one which gave the best effect was
very like the ellipse in section, though not the same ellipse
that was and still is, used by some of the English bell found-
ers. And after further experiments with slightly varying
shapes, I came to the conclusion that the following is the
best shape for large bells on the 13 scale of thickness."—See
Fig. 15.

Divide the diameter of the bell mouth into 24 equal parts.
Then the inside curve is the quarter of an ellipse whose ma-
jor semi-axis A, C, is 14 parts of the diameter, and the
minor semi-axis B, C, is 6 parts of the diameter.

The outside curve cannot, of course, be a single curve,
but must be an empirical curve made in such a way that it
will give what has been found to be the best proportions for
thickness throughout. As the thickness of the waist of the

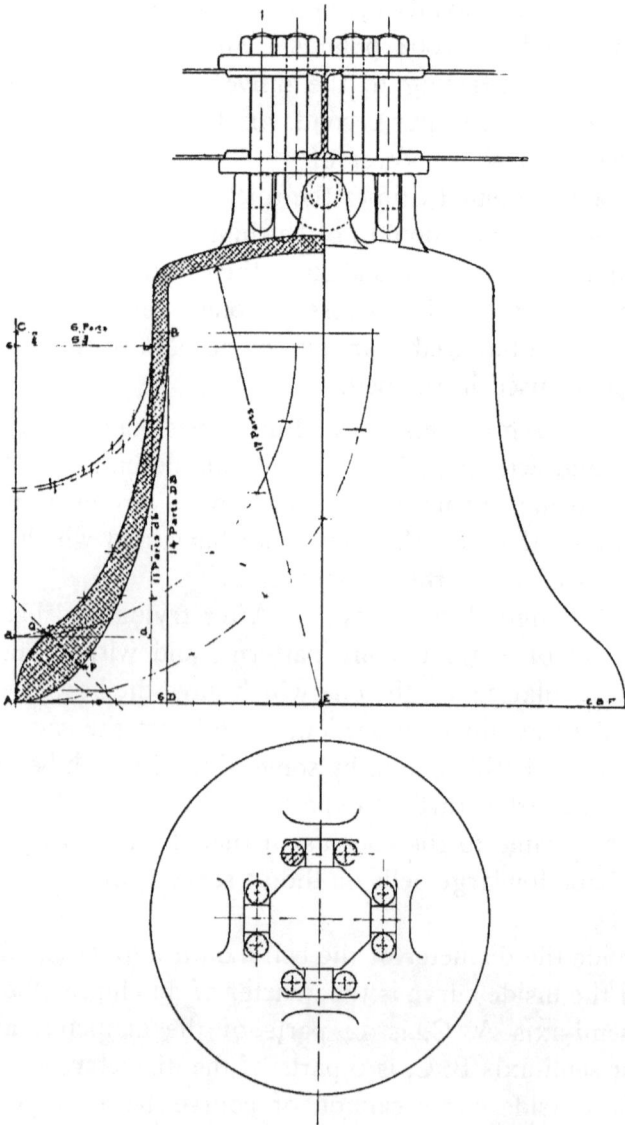

Fig. 15. Method of designing bells.

bell, is to be one-third of the sound bow P, Q, which is one-thirteenth of the diameter b, must be one-thirty-ninth or two-thirds of a "part" outside of B. It is necessary to put the minor axis c b, one-half "part" below C B, in order to make the curve come right at the mouth of the bell. c b, and c a, are the semi-axes of the outer curve, the lower part, a R, is useless and the remaining curve is made up as follows: Draw s Q P 4, to the point 4, in the base line, and make P Q, one-thirteenth of the diameter of the bell; with radius of 3½ or 4 "parts", draw the arc A Q, the curve Q R, is any convenient tangent curve. The top is drawn as a circular arc varying from 16½ to 18 "parts", with E, as a center, the connecting part between the top and the waist is a cylinder.

The composition recommended for the metal is 13 parts copper to 4 parts of tin, by weight, which would be written as a chemical compound: ($Cu_6 Sn_2$.)

Another formula for the curves of bells which gives a taller and thinner bell but of practically the same weight for similar diameters, and thickness at the sound-bow, is as follows: Make the line, f a, Fig. 16 equal to the desired diameter, and the center line, C C, perpendicular to f a. Divide f a, into 10 equal parts. Parallel to the center line C C, draw the line, b, making the distance from b, to C, equal to 2½ "parts" so that the diameter of the "waist" of the bell is one-half that of the mouth. From a, as center, and with a radius of eight "parts" describe an arc cutting the line, b, at the point 8; draw the line, a 8, and divide it into eight "parts" 1, 2, 3, etc. Through these points draw the ordinates perpendicular to, a 8, and make them equal to the length given in the following table:

Length of ordinate through point	I — 0.41 part.
"   "   "   "   "   2   0.86   "
"   "   "   "   "   3   1.02   "
"   "   "   "   "   4 = 1.00   "
"   "   "   "   "   5 = 0.87   "
"   "   "   "   "   6 = 0.66   "
"   "   "   "   "   7 = 0.39   "
"   "   "   "   "   8 = 0.09   "

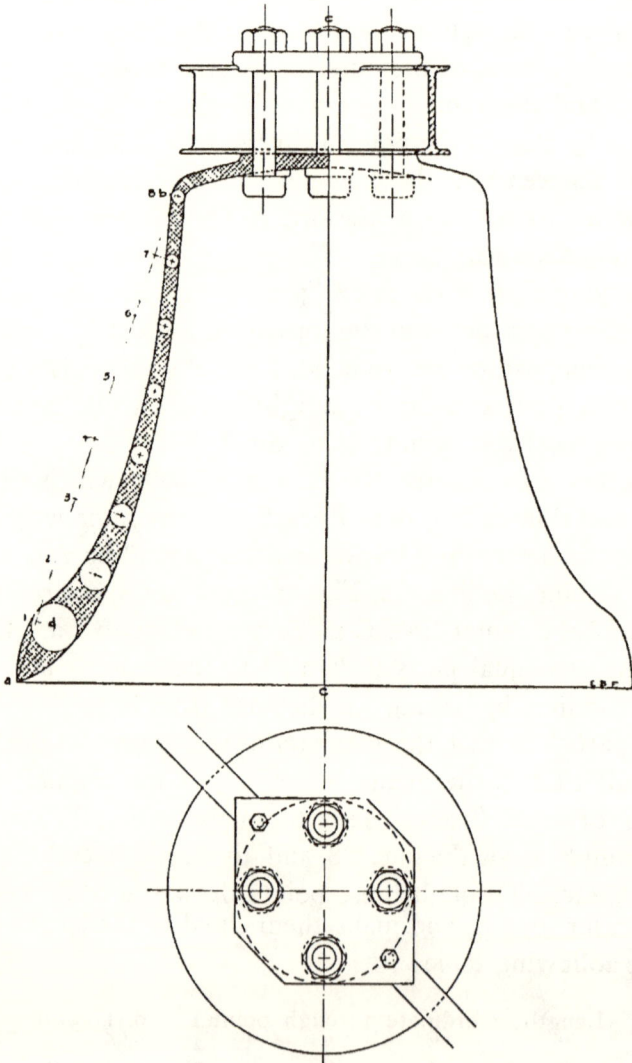

Fig. 16. Second method of designing bells.

These distances locate the centers of circles whose diameters are based upon the desired thickness of the bell at the sound bow. If the same scale of thickness used in the first formula is adhered to, viz: t=one-thirteenth of the diameter of the bell at its mouth then the diameter of the circle, d, on ordinate, 1, will equal one-thirteenth of the line, f a, and with the diameter of d, as a scale make the diameters of the circles on the other ordinates according to the following table:

Diameter of circle on ordinate	1	=		d
" " " "	2	=	0.653	"
. " " " "	3	=	0.4;4	"
" " " "	4	=	0 380	"
ι. " " "	5	=	0.327	"
" " " "	6	=	0.291	"
" " " "	7	=	0.279	"
" " " "	8	=	0.267	"

Draw a curve tangent to these circles and finish the curve from d, to a, in a similar way to that given in the preceding formula. The curve of the crown may also be found in the same way.

No provision is made for a tongue as bells intended for service with a clock should not be rung.

Two forms of crowns are shown.

Fig. 17 shows the detail of the dial, dial gears, universal joint and expansion joint, together with the inside counter weight for the minute hand. This counter balance should be a small weight on a long arm, rather than a heavy weight on a short arm, for, the nearer the length of the arm carrying the weight approaches that of the minute hand, the more perfect the balance.

To balance the minute hand, it should be mounted upon its arbor, together with the counter-weight arm and tested on the balancing-ways, shifting the counter-weight until a perfect balance is obtained; mark the position of the weight on its lever, then when these parts are assembled you are sure the balance is perfect.

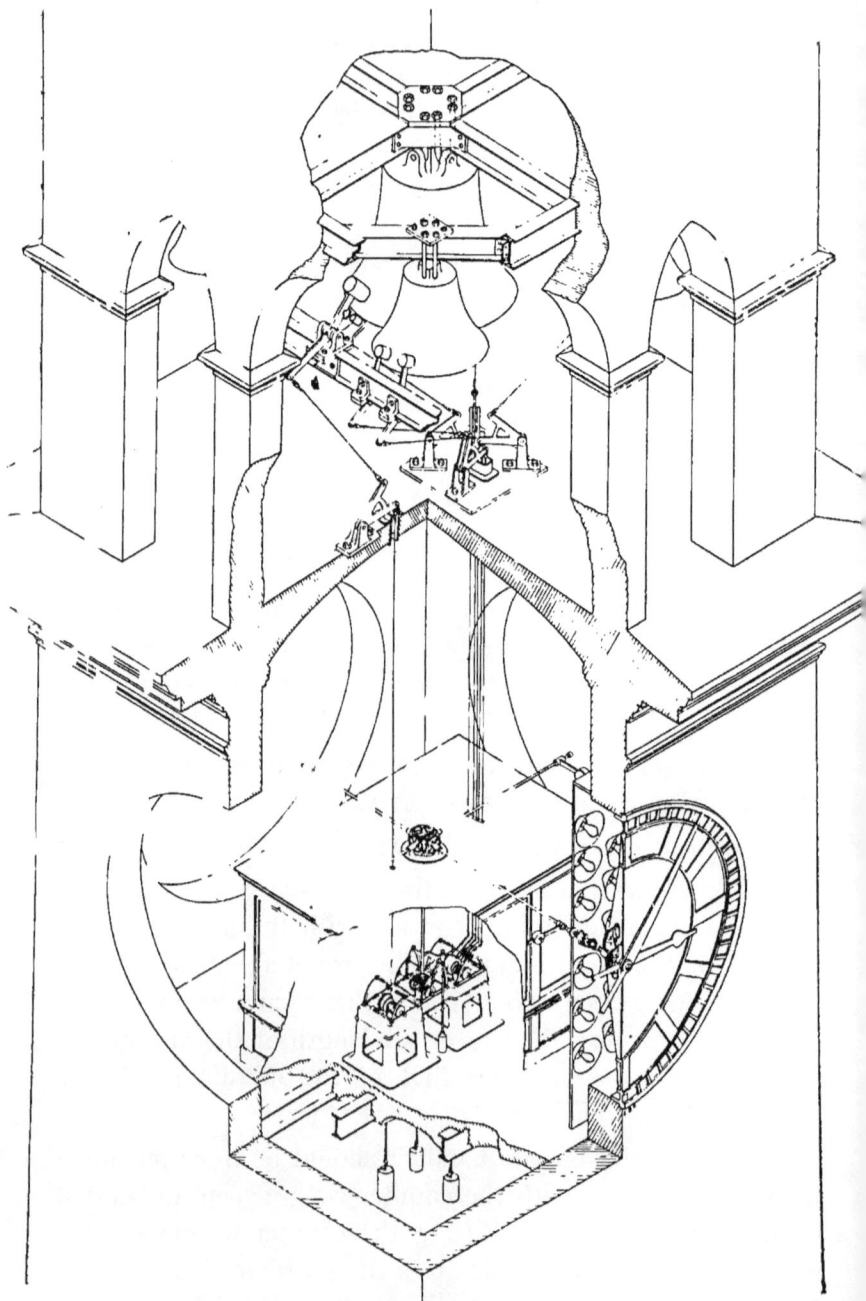

Fig. 18. Sectional view of clock and bells.

Before using the balancing ways, see that the longitudinal and transverse spirit levels show the bubble in the center; if they do not, set the adjusting screws up or down until you have a perfectly level table.

The visible counter weights of the hour and minute hands are of copper, together with the hands so that they can be brazed together securely, and also, because copper is the only thing that will not corrode badly under exposure to the weather.

Just a word in closing in regard to towers : It is quite important that it should be known before the architect designs the tower for a building whether a clock and bells are to be placed in it or not. The clock room and therefore the dials should be below the bells, for greater stability; and large enough to give space in which to enclose the clock by itself, and still leave room to inspect it from all sides.

The bell chamber should be as large as it is possible to make it, as the bells always sound better. Another important point is the windows; in a good many cases, the full tone and vibration of the bell cannot be obtained because the bell is hung too low. They must at least be hung above the sills of the windows. Louvres or overlapping boards to keep out the rain are another source of failure to get the best results from a bell.

www.ingramcontent.com/pod-product-compliance
Lightning Source LLC
Chambersburg PA
CBHW021204090426
42740CB00008B/1226